HASTINGS AND NEIGHBOURHOOD

WALTER HIGGINS

Published by
This edition copyright © 2025 by Zinc Read
Design and setting By Zinc Read
Email- zincread@gmail.com
ISBN- 978-93-7103-662-7

CONTENTS

HASTINGS

Hastings is the gateway into an enchanted garden.

Between the hills and the sea it lies--the most romantic province in this England of ours. Scarcely a place in it seems to belong to this present: from end to end it is built up almost entirely of memories. The very repetition of the names--Rye, Winchelsea, Pevensey, Battle, Bodiam, Hurstmonceux--conjures up the past in all its magnificence and all its sadness. Nowhere in so small a space shall you find so many monuments to the greatness of England's former days, to the imperishable glory of her people; nowhere in our coasts shall you find a stretch of land so crowded with the ghosts of dead men and dead empires.

If for this alone, the territory, no matter how ill-favoured and unattractive, would be worth visiting and revisiting. But there is yet another call--that of the intrinsic beauty of the country-side. And the call here is insistent. Hills and the sea; great folding downs and little valleys dropping fatness; immense stretches of lonely marsh and the nestling charms of copse-hidden villages; gentlest of streams slipping lazily through peacefullest of domains; wildest of breakers spending themselves at the base of steep tawny cliffs. Thus is the land compact. One is always reminded of a passage from Mark Twain: "That beauty which is England is alone; it has no duplicate. It is made up of very simple details, just grass, and trees, and shrubs, and roads, and hedges, and gardens, and houses, and churches, and castles, and here and there a ruin, and over all a mellow dreamland of history. But its beauty is incomparable and all its own." And search where you will--north, south, east, west--nowhere can you come upon a spot to which these words might with greater fitness be applied; for this sequestered little area is the microcosm of England.

Despite its wilderness of bricks and mortar, Hastings itself is, under certain conditions, a place by no means unbeautiful. Possibly it is from the sea that it appears in happiest mood. One can take a boat on a high summer's morning, when the sun is shining gaily on its steep grass-capped cliffs, its fragment of castle ruin, its red and blue-grey roofs, when the sea is mazing away into every tint of emerald and sapphire. Then it is a place fair to behold and pleasing to remember. Or one can clamber to the top of the castle hill, and, Janus-like, comprehend the town in its entirety--eastwards the old town and the Past; westwards the modern watering-place and the Future. Then it is a place for soliloquy and moralizing.

Of the very early history of Hastings we know practically nothing, save that it seems to have been for many years a place apart. Shut off from the west by the invious flats of Pevensey, then one vast network of lagoons: from the east by the greater marsh of Romney; secluded on the north by the grey mystery of Andredesweald, which in those days came as far south as the top of Fairlight Hill, the people experienced a certain splendid isolation. So much so, in fact, that in the early records it was quite customary to refer to them as a race apart, as distinct as either of their nearest neighbours, the Jutes of Kent or the Saxons of Sussex. "And all Kent and Sussex and Hastings" was a phrase running easily from the pens of ancient chroniclers.

No one knows their origin. There was a tribe of Hastengi dwelling on the seaboard between the Elbe and what is now Denmark, having as a chieftain one Haesten, a piratical Dane, with whose name that of the town is often linked (erroneously, say some). In all probability, following on some raid rather more extensive and successful than usual, a party of these Hastengi came by this district as an allotment, and chose to settle here, bringing over their families and herds. Maybe thus the town was originated.

One of their earliest tasks, doubtless, was the construction of a stronghold, either the strengthening of an existing British earthwork or the formation of an entirely new one. The conditions of life demanded that they should possess such a fortification, a place which should be at once the residence of the chief and a refuge for the people in time of danger. And thus it happened that ere long there came into existence the Hastinga-ceastre, mention of which is made in the Anglo-Saxon Chronicle in 1050: "A little before that [the murder of Beorn by Sweyn] the men of Hastinga-ceastre and thereabouts won two of his ships with two of their ships and slew all the men and brought the ships to Sandwich to the King". But prior to 1050 the town must have attained to a considerable maritime strength and commercial eminence, for in 924 Athelstan founded a mint here. The site of this successful Saxon town and harbour is a matter of conjecture; only the hurrying sea knows where it lies.

History proper begins with the coming of the Norman adventurer, although, singularly enough, that worthy paid little attention to the town. Landing at Pevensey on 28th September, 1066, William made his way to Hastinga-ceastre, which he occupied without much show of resistance (despite the picture of burning houses in the Bayeux Tapestry), for the ships had gone north with Harold, and the folks around had neither the means nor the mind to fight. He stayed in the district a fortnight, scouring round for provisions and terrorizing the natives. During that time he set to work to build some sort of a castle, probably on or near the spot where the ancient camp had stood, and where later the Castle proper eventually rose. This we gather from the Bayeux Tapestry, which depicts the digging and timbering of a makeshift stronghold. On 14th October William marched northwards to meet Harold, and the famous Battle of Hastings, or Senlac, was fought.

Thence onward the town seems to have had a very chequered career. Previous to the coming of the Normans the encroachments of the sea and the gradual silting up of the old harbour (wherever it was) had rendered necessary the laying down of a new town in a securer place, and in all probability the building of the town between the east and west cliffs was in that way begun--at a spot far to the south of the present Old Town, of course. The township thus commenced was the *New Burgh* afterwards mentioned in Domesday Book, and placed by William under the jurisdiction of his kinsman, Robert, Count of Eu, and of the Abbot of Fecamp.

The Norman occupation heralded a period of prosperity, for everything was done by William to foster good relationship between the kingdom and the duchy. The continual passage of the monks between France and England, the importation of Caen stone for the building of the abbey (done until similar stone was discovered near at hand), made for commercial growth and stimulated that shipbuilding industry which the proximity of Andredesweald rendered possible. Robert of Eu at once replaced the hastily-formed wooden fortress by a small stone castle, and this was added to from time to time. And so the gradual progress went on till the days of the completion of the Abbey in the reign of the Red King: when Hastings reached its heyday.

Not long, however, did it remain thus in the full flush of existence, for from the time of Stephen onwards it began steadily to decay. Why Hastings ever was the premier port of the Cinque Ports Confederacy it is difficult to say. There were, as the name suggests, five towns--Hastings, Sandwich, Dover, Romney, and Hythe; and in addition there were Winchelsea and Rye, which differed merely in name, being called the Antient Towns. If Hastings were ever the most successful of these, it soon yielded pride of place to its neighbour and rival, Winchelsea. The sovereigns, especially the Angevins, gradually transferred their attentions to the more easterly rivals, proffering no royal aid even when Hastings suffered badly. Slowly, therefore, but certainly, the town sank to an insignificant position, with just here and there a tiny patch of more glorious life; and it revived again only as a result of one of the vagaries of fashion.

It was about 1750 that it took on its second lease of life, soon after the time when Brighton emerged from the obscurity of a small fishing-village to form the fashionable watering-place. Society doctors about that time discovered and began to recommend the advantages of sea-bathing; and, the vogue spreading, Hastings began rapidly to extend. When the Duke of Wellington brought his wife hither in 1806 there were less than four thousand inhabitants; but little by little the cosy valley, where the old town had so long nestled, ceased to be big enough, so that the town overflowed its confines; and eventually the modern resort commenced to flourish, west of the Castle hill--like a garish fungoid growth at the end of some fallen monarch of the forest. It was this modern development that excited the bitterness of Charles Lamb when he wrote his well-known tirade: "I love town or country; but this detestable Cinque Port is neither.... There is no sense of home at Hastings. It is a place of fugitive resort, an heterogeneous assemblage of sea-mews and stockbrokers, Amphitrites of the town, and misses that coquet with the Ocean. If it were what it was in its primitive state, and what it ought to have remained, a fair, honest fishing-town, and no more, it were something--with a few straggling fishermen's huts scattered about, artless as its cliffs, and with their materials filched from them, it were something. I could abide to dwell with Meshech, to assort with fisher-swains, and smugglers.... But it is the visitants from town, that come here to say that they have been here, with no more relish of the sea than a pond-perch or a dace might be supposed to have, that are my aversion.... What can they want here? What mean these scanty book-rooms--marine libraries as they entitle them--if the sea were, as they would have us believe, a book to read strange matter in? What are their foolish concert-rooms, if they come, as they would fain be thought to do, to listen to the music of the waves? All is false and hollow pretension. They come because it is the fashion, and to spoil the nature of the place."

HASTINGS CASTLE

A fragment of the castle alone remains, grimly clinging to the edge of the cliff.

(*See page 13*)

As we stroll about the streets of Hastings of to-day, it is difficult, nay, it is impossible, to conjure up the past, to people these hills and dales with the ghosts of days long since gone. True, there is the Castle ruin, grimly clinging to the edge of the cliff; else there is little but aggressive modernity. Such haven as there is now gives cause rather for ridicule than pride. Few, standing at the Albert Memorial, could ever conceive that here in this Priory valley was at one time the great Port, protected on the east by the Castle hill, on the west by the White Rock, and flushed from the north by the Old Roar River. Well might our old Sussex poet, James Howell, sing:

"Thou old sea-town, crouching beneath the rocks
Like a strong lion waiting for his prey!
Where are thy river, harbour, and the docks
In which the navy of Old England lay?
Why didst thou slumber, when in Pevensey Bay
The Normans' mighty host profaned our soil,
When thou, the Cinque-Port Queen, didst hold the key
Which locked the sea-gates of this freedom-isle?"

Who, standing towards the south of the old town, where now are those black, bill-plastered structures famed as "the fishermen's huts", could call to mind a great wall with a gate and portcullis defending the town on the seaward side? Yet a writer as late as 1828 could say: "Hastings was formerly defended, towards the sea, by a wall, which extended from the castle cliff across the hollow in which the town lies, to the east cliff.... A very small portion of this wall still exists, and may be traced near the Bourne's mouth, where there was a portcullis or gate; a considerable part of it is stated to have remained about forty years since." (William Herbert, the unacknowledged author of "*The History and Antiquities of the Town and Port of Hastings*", by W. G. Moss, draughtsman to H.R.H the Duke of Cambridge.)

Now all has gone. Only the town remains much as before. The description penned in 1828 (*ibid.*)--"The town consists principally of two streets, High Street, and All Saints Street, each about half a mile in length, running parallel nearly north and south, and separated by a rivulet, called the Bourne, which runs into Hastings in a narrow and inconsiderable stream, and empties itself into the sea. These narrow streets are intersected by various smaller ones, or, more properly speaking, alleys, which contain the dwellings of the fishermen and other poor inhabitants of the place"--might well serve for the present day, save that the inconsiderable Bourne has now entirely disappeared. For the rest, a few old timbered houses, the two churches, All Saints and St.

Clements, one on each slope, form, with the Castle, the sum total of the tangible reminders of ancient days.

Nor has the town many definite associations as far as personalities go. True, Titus Oates was baptized here in 1619, when his father was rector of All Saints, and was himself curate in 1674; but the town can scarcely be proud of him. One of the few old timbered houses in All Saints Street is pointed out as the home of the mother of Sir Cloudesley Shovell, but the only evidence in support of the claim is the following extract (generally discredited) from De la Prynne's diary: "I heard a gentleman say, who was in the ship with him six years ago, that as they were sailing over against the town of Hastings in Sussex, Sir Cloudesley called out: 'Pilot, put near; I have a little business on shore.' They came to a little house--'Come,' says he, 'my business is here; I came on purpose to see the good woman of this house.' Upon which they knocked at the door, and out came a poor old woman, upon which Sir Cloudesley kissed her, and then, falling down on his knees, begged her blessing, and called her mother."

Coventry Patmore and Sir John Moore both lived in the town for a time. Otherwise the famous folk have for the most part been visitors. The Duke of Wellington, then Major-General Wellesley, came hither with his bride in 1806, he being then in charge of some twelve thousand soldiers encamped near by. In August, 1814, Byron stayed for a period. "I have been renewing my acquaintance with my old friend Ocean," he wrote, "and I find his bosom as pleasant a pillow for one's head in the morning as his daughters of Paphos could be in the twilight. I have been swimming and eating turbot and smuggling neat brandies and silk handkerchiefs, and walking on cliffs and tumbling down hills, and making the most of the *dolce far niente* of the last fortnight." Thomas Hood spent his honeymoon in the town about a decade later. Garrick, while staying at East Cliffe House, planted in the garden a slip from Shakespeare's mulberry-tree.

West of Hastings, and now merging into it, is the town of St. Leonards. It was founded in 1828 by a Mr. Burton, and took its name from the sixth-century hermit after whom the well-known forest and a number of churches round about were called. Here, at St. Leonards, Thomas Campbell, the poet, lived, and his well-known "Address to the Sea", commencing: "Hail to thy face and odours, glorious Sea!" was inspired by the view from this point. If ever the town needed a testimonial it could scarcely find better than the following passage from Theodore Hook: "From the meditation in which he was absorbed, Jack [Bragg] was roused upon his arrival at the splendid creation of modern art and industry, St. Leonards, which perhaps affords one of the most beautiful proofs of individual taste, judgment and perseverance that our nation exhibits. Under the superintendence of Mr. Burton, a desert has become a thickly peopled town. Buildings of an extensive nature and most elegant character rear their heads where but lately the barren cliffs presented their sandy fronts to the storm and wave, and rippling stream and hanging groves adorn the vale which a few years since was a sterile and shrubless ravine." But perhaps the eulogy must not be taken too seriously.

HASTINGS AND ST. LEONARDS FROM THE CASTLE

West of Hastings, and now merging into it, is the town of St. Leonards, "the splendid creation of modern art and industry. Buildings of an extensive nature and most elegant character rear their heads where but lately the barren cliffs presented their sandy fronts to the storm and wave."

(*See page 16*)

Taken together, Hastings and St. Leonards form a typical modern watering-place,--with the quieter portion to the west, as is usual on the south coast. Here, as an old guide book puts it, "every reasonable wish may be gratified, whether the object of the visitant be health or pleasure". And certainly the place does offer a fine selection of attractions. For your more strenuous visitor there are ample facilities for golf, tennis, swimming, &c.; for your ardent angler there is the unique combination of good deep-sea and river fishing; for your artist or photographer there are countless objects of beauty and historical interest. For those who are content merely to idle away the time amid beautiful surroundings there are the magnificent public gardens,--Alexandra Park, Gensing Gardens, and St. Leonards Gardens. Few towns in England can boast so rich a possession as the park, with its lake, its woodland glades, its fine stretches of greenest turf, its indescribably beautiful flowers; and few municipalities realize so adequately the value of such a possession, if one may judge by the care bestowed upon it.

ST. LEONARDS GARDENS

Few towns in England can boast so rich a possession as the park, with its lake, woodland glades, and beautiful flowers.

(*See page 17*)

However, the surroundings of Hastings must still be its greatest asset. To quote once more the grandiloquent old guide book,--"The vicinity of the town abounds with delightful rides and walks; the pleasantness and diversified character of which it is impossible not to admire; and these are not only of a description superior, perhaps, to what are to be found in almost any other part of the coast, but so numerous as to afford that change which prevents the satiety arising from repetition".

Still farther west lies Bexhill, a typically modern seaside resort. Then follows a considerable stretch of meadow land, and at the other side the first of the romantic centres in this cradle of English history.

PEVENSEY AND HURSTMONCEUX

In all this storied region there is no spot so rich in memories as Pevensey (or Pemsey, as it is called locally). Before such ancient settlements as Rye and Winchelsea were dreamed of, while yet Hastings was the merest collection of barbarian huts, Pevensey, or rather its Roman predecessor, Anderida, was a fortified place with all the ebb and flow of a flourishing life.

Like Winchelsea, it has seen great changes--not quite so tragic perhaps, but no less momentous--and like Winchelsea, too, in its tide of fortune or disaster, it has been at the idle mercy of the fickle sea. Where now--from the Channel inland for three or four miles--stretches a wide plain, centuries ago the sea went on its way, reaching inland as far as Hailsham, and leaving Pevensey and other "eys"--Horseye, Chilleye, Rickney--islanded in its midst. In those days Pevensey served a double purpose: it was an island stronghold and a port--a gate to shut out and a gateway to welcome the alien mariner, according to his intentions and its own will. Then the waters of the Channel receded, and the puissant fortress, robbed of its vital strength, sprawled helplessly at the mercy of any Philistine invader.

It has had just this much of compensation: through its centuries of serviceable isolation it has seen real life as a castle--withstood sieges, beaten off marauding foes, taken sides in internal strife--and in that it has had the cry over the most of our Sussex fortresses.

Originally a Celtic stronghold, it became, by reason of its unique situation, the Anderida of the Romans, a fortified enclosure following roughly the shape of the knoll on which it stood. This was in the third century. Two hundred years later, when the Romans had departed and left behind an enervated British race, the invading Saxons descended on the stronghold, put to death every Briton they could find, and destroyed all traces of the Roman settlement within the walls. For centuries after this the enclosure was unoccupied; but the port continued its activities, for we read that in the years 1042 and 1049 Earl Godwin and his sons, Sweyn and Harold, fell upon the place with sword and torch, and carried off many ships.

But its real value as a castle site was only completely realized when, in September of the year 1066, William the Norman landed there with his hordes of mailed warriors. He straightway gave the derelict to his half-brother, Robert of Mortain, who proceeded to erect a Norman fortress at the east end of the enclosure, using the strengthened Roman walls as an outer line of defence. To this was added, two centuries later, a strong inner keep.

Since the time of the Norman landing Pevensey seems to have sustained at least four earnest sieges. The first took place in 1088, when Odo, Bishop of Bayeux, and supporter of Robert of Normandy, defended the castle against the Red King: the second in 1147, when the place was held for the Empress Matilda against King Stephen; and in both of these cases the defenders were compelled by famine to surrender. The third important attack was that of 1264, following the battle of Lewes, when Simon de Montfort and the Barons sought in vain to reduce a garrison of obstinate Royalists. It was during this particular siege that the larger gap in the original Roman wall was initiated. The fourth and last storming happened during the Wars of the Roses, when Lady Pelham, a stanch supporter of the Lancastrian cause, successfully held out against a force of local followers of Richard of York.

After that the glory of the place departed, and it became a State prison, wherein were incarcerated such illustrious personages as Edward, Duke of York; James the First of Scotland; and Queen Joan of Navarre, wife of Henry the Fourth. From the days of the seventh Henry onwards it gradually fell into decay; and its present dilapidated condition is due not so much to the violence of the sieges as to the habit of the local gentry of using the remains as a handy quarry for house-building purposes. For the presence of any remains at all our thanks are due to that much-reviled thing the Spanish Armada. In the year previous to the sailing of the fleet, orders were given for the complete restoration or total demolition of the castle. Happily, in the general confusion of the time, the instructions seem to have been forgotten. Pevensey now is one of the most picturesque spots in the south of England. The knoll on which it stands is sufficiently high to give the castle a dignified appearance, as it rises up out of the encompassing marshes; and yet there is none of that grim, forbidding aspect generally so noticeable about castles perched on an eminence. Rather is there about these ivy-mantled walls an atmosphere of sunlit serenity quite out of keeping with the story of the place. Around the little hill still stretch those amazing ancient Roman walls, with but two considerable breaches. These walls for the most part fail to get the attention they deserve. Visitors enter the little western gate and pass across the meadow--once the outer ward--and so come to the mediaeval castle; but the outer walls are nearly a thousand years older and of transcendent interest. What magnificent masons those old

Romans were! And what a secret they must have possessed for the making of mortar and cement! In several places here the cement has endured through all these hundreds of years, while even the outer stones have crumbled away. At other points, too, the actual marks of the masons' tools are visible in the ancient mortar.

PEVENSEY CASTLE FROM THE MEADOWS

Through centuries of serviceable isolation it has seen real life as a castle--withstood sieges, beaten off marauding foes, and taken sides in internal strife.

(*See page 23*)

At the eastern end of the enclosure is the castle itself, with a reed-grown moat on the northern and western sides. Most of this ruin dates back only to the time of Edward the First, for the original Norman fabric suffered too many sieges to endure in any completeness. One of the great towers flanking the main gateway still stands, but the other, like the drawbridge, has long since disappeared; three others project from the wall at various intervals. Inside, very little remains. Fragmentary ruins reveal the original site of the keep: the extent of the chapel may be traced on the sward. But, for all the scarcity of definite relics, the place is one to linger in and conjure up the past, when these grass-grown spaces were instinct with a hurrying life, when the meadows where now the cattle browse were filled with anxious faces and beating hearts.

Pevensey can own to one famous son at least, Andrew Borde, a man of many parts. Carthusian monk, physician to Henry the Eighth, litterateur, poor Borde died a prisoner in the Fleet Prison in 1549. He was one of those unfortunates who seem never to do or say the right thing at the right time. Born at the vicarage early in the sixteenth century, he developed a turn for jesting, and it proved his undoing, for bishops and kings had not his lively wit, and failed lamentably to appreciate what was at once his gift and his failing. To his ready pen have been ascribed the immortal epic "Tom Thumb", and the oft-told "Merry Tales of the Wise Men of Gotham"--the latter collected and put into literary form from the oral traditions of the country-side.

Just up under the eastern wall of the castle is the so-called Mint House, where Borde is reputed to have spent many of his days. It was an interesting old place, with its panelled walls and numerous passages; but it has now been rendered quite impossible by reason of its conversion into a glorified old curiosity shop with a heterogeneous collection of antiques. Other delightful houses there are, too, in this double village of Pevensey and Westham, straggling away at either side of the castle--low, picturesque timbered dwellings, at once the delight and despair of would-be artists. At Westham is a noble old church, the first built by the Conqueror, with remnants of the original Norman fabric still serving their purpose.

Striking east from the castle, the way out to Hurstmonceux lies down through the village street, with the sea away to the right and the marsh to the left. All along the coast here stand the Martello towers, monuments to the hysteria of a former day. Poor Cobbett, in his *Rural Rides*, could scarce find words bitter enough for these works. "To think that I should be destined to behold these monuments of the wisdom of Pitt and Dundas and Perceval! Good G--! Here they are, piles of brick in a circular form about three hundred feet (guess) circumference at the base, about forty feet high, and about one hundred feet circumference at the top.... Cannons were to be fired from the top of these things, in order to defend the country against the French Jacobins! I think I could have counted along here upwards of thirty of these ridiculous things, which, I dare say, cost five, perhaps ten, thousand pounds each: and one of which was, I am told, *sold* on the coast of Sussex, the other day, for two hundred pounds...." Some have now been dismantled, having been rendered useless or dangerous by the encroachments of the sea. Here and there is to be found one providing habitation for a fisherman or a coastguard, or let out for the purpose of a summer residence to some more than usually enterprising holiday-maker.

As soon as the water of Pevensey Haven is crossed, the way to Hurstmonceux turns sharply to the north; and thence onward the road is a perfectly flat one, winding in and out across the levels with seeming aimlessness. Ahead, visible nearly all the way, the castle nestles among the low hills that break sharply away from the flats, outposts of the uplands of that same sandstone Forest Ridge which presses on eastwards to form the cliffs beyond Hastings. On either side, away to the distant hills, stretch the greenest of meadows, intersected by innumerable watercourses, with but a few stunted thorns and an occasional tuft of rushes to break the trackless level. Here the soft-eyed Sussex beasts browse knee-deep in luxuriant pasturage. It is a lonely spot, a place of drowsy solitude, where the plaintive call of the plover seems the most natural melody. Yet, on a spring morning, when great white clouds ride across the clear blue sky, when the thorn is in bloom, and every ditch is brocaded with the gold of myriad kingcups, then, indeed, it is a place of indescribable sweetness.

Built at the time of the "last of the barons", Hurstmonceux marked the transition in domestic architecture from the heavily-defended fortress to the comfortable and luxurious manor-house. As early as the reign of Edward the Third attempts had been made to combine the strength of massive masonry with the convenience of more sumptuous apartments, such castles as Raglan and Warwick leading the way. We have only to stroll round the present remains to find ample evidence of this double service. The great arched gateway and battlemented walls, the machicolated octagonal towers, the moat and drawbridge, the loopholes for cross-bows, the oeillets for the matchlock guns,--all witness to the one purpose; while the size and number of the windows in the dwelling-rooms quite well testify to the other.

In these days the ruined castle is a place of great beauty. Time has dealt less hardly with it than with some. The colour of the huge red-brick front has been softened down by wind and rain to a restful mellow tint in full harmony with the sombre green of the overhanging masses of ivy;

and, though the broken walls with their towers and half-towers still have a martial air, they have lost much of their severity of outline.

In the full flush of its being it was a magnificent structure. Just inside the great gateway there was a courtyard, generally known as the "Green Court", surrounded by the cloisters. Just beyond this stood the great dining-hall, a spacious chamber, 54 feet long and 28 wide, with massive timbered roof and tiled floor; and, opening from it, the Pantry Court, from which again a paved passage led to the garden. The east side of the castle included the principal dwelling-apartments,--the enormous drawing-room, where Grinling Gibbons's vine, a masterpiece of carving, spread its magnificence over the walls and ceiling; the chapel, extending up through the two stories; and, on the upper floor, the "Ladies' Bower" with its peculiar oriel window--a room wherein, tradition says, one of the fair daughters of Hurstmonceux was starved to death in her twenty-first year. On the west were the domestic apartments, among them the great kitchen and bakehouse, with an oven in which, it was declared, a coach and horses might easily turn. On the upper floor, lighted by the open space of the Green Court, were the Bethlehem chambers, otherwise the guest-rooms, and the Green Gallery, a room filled with pictures and hung with green cloth. One old writer speaks of these upper rooms as "sufficient to lodge a garrison"; and adequate provision would seem to have been necessary, for in its heyday Hurstmonceux had many and illustrious visitors. Everything seems to have been done on such a lavish scale that we are fully prepared for such interesting details as the record that at the marriage of Grace Naylor "butts of beer were left standing at the park gates for the refreshment of chance passers-by"; also that twenty old female retainers were kept constantly employed at the weeding and tidying of the Green and other courtyards.

For long it was a mere skeleton, at the mercy of nature and man. As late as 1752 Horace Walpole could write of it in a letter to his friend Richard Bentley: "It was built in the reign of Henry VI, and is as perfect as the first day. It does not seem to have ever been quite finished, or at least that age was not arrived at the luxury of whitewash, for almost all the walls are in their native brick-hood." And yet, despite Mr. Walpole's assertions as to its continued perfectness, so soon after this as 1777 the castle was dismantled. The truth is: if the castle has escaped the general fate of this region and avoided the scourge of the invader, it has nevertheless suffered much at the hands of its friends. In the year mentioned the owner was a Mrs. Henrietta Hare, ancestor of the author of *Memorials of a Quiet Life,* a volume which deals very faithfully with this ancient fabric. This lady, desiring to use the materials for the construction of a new mansion on a higher site, called in the arch-vandal Wyatt, and he (to quote Augustus Hare's *Memorials*) "declared that the castle was in a hopeless state of dilapidation, though another authority had just affirmed that in all material points its condition was as good as on the day on which it was built.... The castle was unroofed.... A great sale was held in the park, whither the London brokers came in troops, and lived in an encampment of tents during the six weeks which the sale lasted. Almost everything of value was then dispersed. Mrs. Hare and her husband afterwards resided at Hurstmonceux Place, the new house which Wyatt was commissioned to build, and lived there in such extravagance that they always spent a thousand a year more than their income, large as it was, and annually sold a farm from the property to make up the deficiency. It was a proverb in the neighbourhood at that time that 'people might hunt either Hares or foxes'."

And thus it stood, a ruined shell, until comparatively recent years. The many curious staircases built in the thicknesses of the walls, the secret underground passages, and the general isolation on the edge of the marsh, all contrived to render the ruin an ideal rendezvous for smugglers and a suitable depository for their stores of contraband.

Now, fortunately, the castle is in the hands of one who, appreciating such a possession, is taking steps to prevent any further decay, and with a loving care and a sense of fitness is proceeding with the delicate task of necessary restoration.

BATTLE ABBEY

To Battle is the excursion of paramount interest from the popular point of view. The association with one of the most momentous events in the history of the land, the peculiar entertainment of standing on the actual ground where the battle took place and the "last of the English" fell, the intrinsic pleasure in the inspection of a ruin at once rich in memories and comely in setting,--all contrive to make it the pilgrimage into the country around. Other ruins may surpass it in degree of preservation, in individual reminiscence, in charm of situation, but none, not even Pevensey, can vie with the Abbey in strength of appeal.

It was erected on the actual place of the contest. On the eve of the battle, when the rival forces were assembled and ready for the shock of arms, William, in a sudden fit of piety--or nervousness--made a solemn vow that, should victory be his, he would found a mighty church, in token of his thankfulness for the Divine intervention. And when it was all over, and the English had fallen, he quickly made good his promise. Practical men came to him urging the unsuitable nature of the site, high up on the hill-side away from all water. Rather would they build down there in the hollow, where the springs ever gushed forth freely. But not so William: the church should rise on the field of blood, and the high altar should mark the spot where his adversary had fallen. And for the matter of water: if that were lacking, well, wine should be more plentiful in the new Abbey than water in other religious houses. Thus came the venerable Abbey of St. Martin into existence.

The story of the battle is perhaps the most fascinating in all our catalogue of worthy fights. When William landed on these shores Harold was at York, recuperating after the superhuman efforts which culminated in the battle of Stamford Bridge, where he entirely defeated an invading force under Harold Haardrada and his own brother, Tostig. He had marched two hundred miles or more to defeat one foe, and it was now necessary for him to carry out a still greater expedition to engage a second. He halted several days in the capital while the process of collecting troops from the midlands and the south went on. At last, on October the twelfth, he moved on to meet William. With him he took but a small army. Had he waited just a short time longer (the delay would not have mattered, for William had no intention of leaving the coast) he could have gathered a force sufficiently large to overwhelm the invaders; but he made the common mistake of holding the enemy too cheaply. A series of forced marches commenced in the hopes of catching William unawares came to nought, owing to the vigilance of the Duke's marauding bands. On the night of the thirteenth he arrived at the fatal hill, and pitched his camp on the site of the present town of Battle.

THE GATEWAY, BATTLE ABBEY

The Abbey was erected on the field of the Battle of Hastings. The gateway was added in 1338 to the work begun by William the Conqueror.

(See page 36)

THE GATEWAY, BATTLE ABBEY

The Abbey was erected on the field of the Battle of Hastings. The gateway was added in 1338 to the work begun by William the Conqueror.

(*See page 36*)

Harold apparently knew this part of Sussex quite well, being the lord of several manors round about; and so his well-chosen ground does not surprise us. A long spur of upland here thrusts out boldly from the main mass of wooded hill-side, and commands a view over a wide stretch of rolling ground away to the sea. On a crest of this spur he ranged his army, with the mailed warriors in front forming a continuous shield-wall.

The descriptions of the night before the battle--all from Norman sources, by the way--make vastly interesting reading. Albeit they vary in certain minor matters, they are in one accord concerning the characters of the rival armies--the drunken English and the pious Normans. The former spent the night in one big carousal--dancing, singing, drinking immense quantities of liquor; the latter devoted their time to prayers and the confession of their sins. And yet, strange to say, the English seem to have been quite fit in the morning, for they put up a remarkably good fight. They held their own through the best part of the day, and in the end were defeated only by their own eagerness.

Hour after hour the Normans surged up the hill, assailing the English position, and again and again were they driven back by the terrible battle-axes of their opponents. So well was Harold's position chosen that they could make little impression; and it is fair to hazard that in the end they would have met with defeat, had not some of the less-disciplined troops forsaken their advantage and impetuously pursued the panic-stricken enemy into the valley below. Here the conditions were different, and the sword was more than a match for the battle-axe and javelin, with the consequence that the rash English were badly cut up. William noticed this, and determined to try the "strategic retreat" on a larger scale. Accordingly one wing--the western--was ordered to turn tail and retire as though in disorder. This they did. The English, lured on by their wily foes, readily gave up their more favourable position, and then, as before, the French turned and engaged them, while a wedge of cavalry inserted itself and harassed them in the rear. This descending movement had left open a considerable portion of the English line, and on this William concentrated the pick of his forces. But still the English fought on stubbornly. In one place they also saw the advantage of the feigned flight, and induced the French cavalry to charge into an unsuspected ravine, whence not a man escaped.

As the shades of evening fell no one might say where the advantage lay: the English shield-wall was broken in places, but it still presented a formidable line; the French still pressed on eagerly. Then to Duke William came the great inspiration which turned the day, and won for him the battle and the crown. So far his archers had done little to justify their presence on the field. Now William saw that if they were ordered to shoot their arrows high into the air these would descend with terrific force upon the heads of the foe, and work great execution. The command was carried out, and one of the first to fall was the English king himself, his right eye pierced by a shaft.

With Harold fell the English fortunes. His soldiers struggled on desperately till night closed down, but their valour was in vain, and after a day's continuous fighting the Normans were left the victors of the field.

Building operations were duly commenced, and proceeded apace. The growing Abbey was richly endowed, and its Superior granted numerous and great privileges. Not, however, till William had been dead some seven years was it finished. Then for several centuries it enjoyed a flourishing existence, extending its scope and increasing its wealth. The great gateway was added in 1338, and was the work of Abbot Retlyng.

The income of the Abbey was enormous, and the wanton generosity of the brothers made Battle a happy hunting-ground for the pilgrims and vagabonds and ne'er-do-wells in the south-east of England. But its long years of prosperity proved its undoing, for slothful ease gave way to greater evils. The great place decayed in every sense, and when, in 1538, Henry's commissioners appeared at its gate, it was in a fit condition to be suppressed. Layton, the chief commissioner, says of it: "So beggarly a house I never see, nor so filthy stuff. I will no 20s. for all the hangings in this house, as the bearer can tell you.... So many evil I never see, the stuff is like the persons"; and he further speaks of the inmates as "the worst that ever I see in all other places, whereat I see specially the blake sort of dyvellyshe monks".

As we pass through the magnificent gateway, worthy indeed to guard the treasure within, our pleasure increases at every step, for though the ruins are but few and fragmentary they are enshrined in that most glorious of settings, a beautiful garden. The great church itself has long since disappeared, for Sir Anthony Browne, to whom the place was given after the visit of the vandal commissioners, saw nothing of worth in it. Just a fragment of the nave wall is pointed out in the woodyard at the back of the modern mansion, and a piece of the cloister arcading on the east side. But we can get a very good idea of its great size from the disposition of the ruins. The spot to which we turn with eagerness is the site of the high altar, the death-place of Harold. It is a spot of beauty now, with its moss-grown stones, its ferns and greenery; and we would fain linger awhile to think on all the Norman invasion brought, all its woes and its brightnesses; but the guide is inexorable: we must pass on with the flock of tourists to view the only considerable remain, the Early English hall, generally known as the Refectory. The walls of this stand roofless to the sky, with a lawn in place of a floor. Below there are three fine vaulted chambers--one, the Scriptorium, with a good geometrical window and a vaulted roof supported by graceful pillars.

But after all we come away with no very clear idea of the place; and perhaps it is as well. Instead, we have a vague, an impressionist picture of flowers and ruins, grey stones mantled with gorgeous blossoms; and over all a brooding serenity.

The pedestrian's route, by which we may either come to Battle or return, passes through Hollington and Crowhurst. At the latter place is one of the most famous yews in the country; at the former is the notorious "Church in the Wood". Just why this little church should ever have attained to its present eminence as a goal of pilgrimage we fail utterly to comprehend. There is nothing remarkable about the edifice itself, either in the way of structure or ornaments; the graveyard is too crowded with the hideous monuments of parvenu strangers to be interesting; the approach is little more than commonplace. Yet for all that, thousands come and go through the summer months, and on fine Sundays the little sanctuary is packed to the door, doubtless to the entire satisfaction of the clergy. Charles Lamb discovered the place many years ago, when the surroundings were rather more favourable; and we should certainly give thanks, for the visit gave rise to an inimitable passage: "It is a very Protestant Loretto, and seems dropt by some angel for the use of the hermit, who was at once parishioner and a whole parish.... It is built to the text of 'two or three are assembled in my name'. It reminds me of the grain of mustard seed. If the glebe land is proportionate, it may yield two potatoes. Tithes out of it could be no more split than a hair. Its first fruits must be its last, for 'twould never produce a couple. It is truly the strait and narrow way, and few there be--of London visitants--that find it.... It is secure from earthquakes, not more from sanctity than size, for 'twould feel a mountain thrown upon it no more than a taper-worm would. Go and see, but not without your spectacles."

ECCLESBOURNE AND FAIRLIGHT

East of the old town is a stretch of cliffs several miles long, made up, like the Forest Ridge, of Lower Cretaceous rocks. Several little wooded valleys extend from the high lands right down to the sea, and two of these have attained to a desirable celebrity under the names of Ecclesbourne and Fairlight Glens.

Many folk, visiting these two spots in August, go away with a feeling of utter disappointment, for the grass is rusty and the place strewn with the indescribable litter of a myriad picnic-parties. But in the spring of the year, when the little watercourse at the bottom is at its fullest, when there are countless primroses beneath the fine old trees, when everything is green down to the water's edge, then do these glens deserve their reputations.

FAIRLIGHT GLEN

In the spring of the year, when the little watercourse is at its fullest, there are countless primroses beneath the fine old trees, and everything is green down to the water's edge.

(*See page 39*)

In Fairlight there are two famous spots--the Dripping Well and the Lovers' Seat. The well, situated at the northern end of the glen, shows a decided tendency to follow the custom of most local waters, but we can nevertheless get some idea of what a pretty little spot it must have been at its best. The Lovers' Seat is a little to the east, high up on the face of a steep, shrub-grown cliff. A large rock overhangs at the top, and beneath is a tiny platform, slowly disappearing. It is a fine place, especially on an early summer morning, when the air is athrob with the tumultuous melody of the birds in the glen below, and the sea birds wheel round the aerie--a place well fitted to stir even Charles Lamb to praise: "Let me hear that you have clambered up to Lovers' Seat; it is as fine in that neighbourhood as Juan Fernandez, as lonely too, when the fishing-boats are not out; I have sat for hours staring upon a shipless sea. The salt sea is never so grand as when it is left to itself." Of course it has a story: what similar romantic spot has not? Doubt has been cast on the veracity; but such pretty tales certainly *ought* to be true.

East of the glen lies Cliff End, where the brown sandstone cliffs dip down sharply once more to the level marshlands. The path thither meanders along the top of the cliffs, now approaching perilously near the edge to give a glimpse of some sweet little hanging dell with trees right down to the waves, now wandering inland a little through acres of bee-thronged gorse and heather. It is such a spot as Richard Jefferies loved: "All warmly lit with sunshine, deep under liquid sunshine like sands under the liquid sea, no harshness of man-made sound to break the isolation amid nature".

Once at Cliff End we marvel, and yet offer up fervent thanks that it is not one of the "show places" of the district. The low rolling hills, having constituted the coast-line for half a dozen miles, at this point break away inland to form a delightful country-side. By so doing they enclose what was formerly a great lagoon or inland sea, having long arms, or fiords, running up into the different river-valleys of Brede, Tillingham, and Rother. Now the sea has gone, and there, in its place, stretch away acres upon acres of marshland, marked out like a piece of old patchwork by the countless watercourses--a place of stressless labour and contentment.

As we stand at this place and gaze out eastwards upon those broad acres of sun-washed, wind-swept meadow-land, where now the cattle and sheep graze peacefully and the shepherd slumbers at his post, it is difficult to realize that here the fishermen once dropped their nets, and the ships of war rode majestically at anchor--ready at any moment to venture forth against marauding foes. Yet Winchelsea, which stands out in the distance--seeming one day miles away and another barely a stone's throw--and Rye, a tiny town, perched on its little hill some three miles farther on, were each ports of the first magnitude--veritable cradles of the navy and the Empire.

From the Cliff End here we have a choice of two routes: either we can proceed by road to Icklesham, a place well worth a visit for the sake of its interesting old church, and then on to Winchelsea; or, better still, we can tramp the few miles beside the old military canal, which serves to link up that town with the sea. This latter is certainly a delightful walk, and well worth the fatigue of an extended effort. As we drop down the slope, we note, on the lower ridges of the hills, Pett, the insignificant village which has given its name to the Level, or tongue of "polder", stretching away to Rye, and extending eastwards into that greater flat, the Romney Marsh; and, farther on, Guestling. Not hastily, however, must Guestling be passed by, for though the village is commonplace enough to the eye, the name is charged with ancient memories. Originally the "Guestling" was a sort of conference between the Ports and distant fishing colonies such as Yarmouth; but gradually it developed into a local Parliament held to settle disputes among the folks of the rival fisher towns as to questions of rights and privileges. It met in the church itself, and possessed a Speaker and something of the paraphernalia of full judicial power. Here is what the good old Jeake says about it in his ancient *History of the Cinque Ports*: "By the same name of *Guestling,* is also a Court called, that consisteth but of *part* of the *Ports* and *two Towns,* as suppose Hastings, Winchelsea, and Rye, raised upon request of one of them; where by consent, and as by brotherly invitation, they appear to agree on something necessary to their respective Towns."

The old canal, like the Martello towers, roused the scorn of Cobbett: "Here is a canal *to keep out the French*; for these armies who had so often crossed the Rhine, and the Danube, were to be kept back by a canal, made by Pitt, thirty feet wide at the most". But despite Cobbett's words it was no mean feat of military engineering for those days, as the following particulars, culled from Horsfield, the old county historian, will show: "The Military Canal, which was cut, during the late war with France, as a protection to the lowlands in the eastern part of this county and the adjoining portion of the county of Kent, by impeding the progress of an enemy, in the event of a landing on this shore, commences at Cliffe End, in the parish of Pett, and following the course of the rising ground, which skirts the extensive flat forming Walland and Romney Marsh, crosses the Roman Road near Hythe, and extends, in nearly a straight direction, along the coast to its termination at Shorne Cliffe, in Kent; a distance of about twenty-three miles. Its breadth is about twenty yards, and its depth three; with a raised bank or redan on the northern side to shelter the soldiery, and enable them to oppose the foe with greater advantage." Now everything is changed; this monument of warlike stupidity has become a haunt of peace. Thus has Time effected another of its little travesties.

Following the reed-grown, bird-haunted waterway, we skirt the peninsula on which the town is perched, and come finally to the foot of the road which winds diagonally up to the Strand Gate. Thus is the town entered by its most beautiful approach.

WINCHELSEA

Every spot in this delectable corner of England--Pevensey, Hurstmonceux, Hastings itself, Bodiam, Rye--is redolent of the triumph of change; but Winchelsea stands before us a perfect memorial to the futility of man's efforts against Nature, a tangible reminder of the irony of Time.

This ancient town, perched, like Rye, on a solitary hillock projecting into the midst of a vast plain, is, despite its years and its ruins, really a *new* Winchelsea. The old town--the city proper--a prosperous place of seven hundred householders and fifty odd inns, lies beneath the ever-changing sea, some two miles (some say, five) south-east of the present site. Serious trouble began in 1250 with a great tempest, concerning which Holinshed writes: "On the first day of October (1250) the moon, upon her change, appearing exceeding red and swelled, began to show tokens of the great tempest of wind that followed, which was so huge and mightie, both by land and sea, that the like had not been lightlie knowne, and seldome, or rather never heard of by men then alive. The sea forced contrarie to his natural course, flowed twice without ebbing, yielding such a rooring that the same was heard (not without great woonder) a farre distance from the shore.... At Winchelsey, besides other hurt that was doone in bridges, milles, breakes, and banks, there were 300 houses and some churches drowned with the high rising of the watercourse." Not even then did the people give in; but from 1250 to 1287 Neptune and other sovereign powers descended mightily on the poor old town, and its tragedy was completed when, during an utterly disastrous tempest, the whole district between Pett and Hythe was inundated.

At this time Edward the First was Warden of the Cinque Ports, and the planning of the new town seems to have been to him and his associates a simple and congenial task. The present triangular plateau was chosen, falling precipitously on three sides, with its narrow end towards Hastings; and the new town was projected and begun on truly magnificent lines. Edward seems to have been quite a pioneer in the modern science of town-planning, for Winchelsea, like several other towns set out by him, was given an oblong shape, and this was divided up into thirty-nine or forty squares by means of wide streets intersecting at right angles.

On the north the town stood upon a cliff overhanging the Brede fiord; on the east the land fell away precipitously to the sea itself. At the north-east and north-west corners of the plateau, roads were made down to the sea, with quays at the bottom of each, and great gates, the Strand and Ferry, at the top. At the land end yet another gate was built, the New, and the extremity protected by a moat and stone walls. A castle was built, and full provision made for the resumption of the commerce of the port.

THE STRAND GATE, WINCHELSEA

Winchelsea stands upon a plateau, at the north-east and north-west corners of which roads were made down to the sea, with quays at the bottom of each, and great gates, the Strand and Ferry, at the top.

(*See page 49*)

The various religious houses were reproduced as in the dead town, and ere long the lusty life of the old place began again in earnest. The town became self-supporting with its shipbuilding and fishing, and its galaxy of representative craftsmen, and offered a splendid channel for trade to and from the mainland. Being a serviceable defensive port, it rehabilitated itself as a rendezvous for the navy, and combined with that importance the added attraction of being the best base on the coast for pirates. So well was the latter occupation organized that we read of one of the mayors of the town--one Robert de Battayle--being caught red-handed and summarily punished for acts of piracy.

And what remains? Very little. At the northern end certain of the spacious streets are inhabited but generally grass-grown. These show the original divisions and dimensions; but southwards and westwards the majestic squares have become merely green fields, until at last the boundaries have been lost altogether. Ancient words of doom ring in our ears as we survey the scene: "Thorns shall come up in her palaces, nettles and brambles in the fortresses thereof.... They shall be left altogether unto the fowls of the mountains and to the beasts of the earth; and the fowls shall summer upon them, and all the beasts of the earth shall winter upon them."

The church, or rather a certain portion of it, still stands, with a generous margin of green surrounding it, and within its walls the fine canopied tomb of Gervase Alard, admiral of the Cinque Ports. A short distance down the road, south-east of the church, is the mansion known as "The Friars": in its beautiful grounds stands practically all that remains of the religious houses--the ivy-grown ruin of the chapel of the Franciscan Monastery. With this mansion and with the brothers Weston, the rogues who dwelt in it, all lovers of Thackeray's *Denis Duval* will doubtless be familiar. The gates of the town still frown down on the approaching roads; but wall, castle, quays, all are gone, and the place is now, to use Wesley's words, "that poor skeleton of ancient Winchelsea".

WINCHELSEA CHURCH

The church, or a certain portion of it, still stands, with a generous margin of green surrounding it, and within its walls the fine canopied tomb of Gervase Alard, Admiral of the Cinque Ports.

(*See page 48*)

And small wonder too, for every hand has been against it. At the time of its building the Black Death made its appearance, destroying countless inhabitants and dispersing the craftsmen. The town was sacked by the French in 1359, when three thousand entered with sword and torch. Again, in 1378, the same catastrophe occurred. In 1449 they visited once more, but did little damage. For by this time another enemy had set to work--the worst enemy of all. The sea, which in its inconstancy had made the new Winchelsea at the expense of the old, was calmly receding and leaving the Antient Town high and dry, with a perpetually increasing bank of shingle in between.

Now, as we stand at the Strand Gate, and watch the sea away to the south, with its ever-changing pageant of azure and amethyst, and as we turn about and enter through the old gate to walk the grass-grown streets, we laugh at Neptune's jest; but there is something tragic in the laughter.

RYE

Rye, as it stands, is the completest place in England. A little conical hill rises abruptly out of the encompassing marshes, and all around that little hill, wherever it can gain secure hold, clings the town. The tall houses rest tier upon tier, as if standing on tiptoe to get a better view of the approaching enemy; and the cobble-paved streets wind in and about, so that every available inch of space may be utilized for house or hanging garden. Crowning it all rises the ancient church with its high red roofs and tower.

RYE

A conical hill rises abruptly out of the encompassing marshes, and all around that little hill, wherever it can gain secure hold, clings the town.

(*See page 50*)

Probably the best approach is from Camber. We can tramp the three long dusty miles of the military road from Winchelsea, catching just a glimpse of the massive, lowlying structure of Camber Castle on the other side of the stream; or else we can take the road to the right, and, sweeping seawards, come round to the castle itself, pausing a while to wander about these walls which have stood the rough usage of the south-westerly gale so well since the time of the eighth Henry. Leaving Camber, the way across to Rye is hazardous. So many waterways intersect the shingly meadows that by the time we come out at the right place an extraordinarily tortuous path has been followed.

The history of Rye is much akin to that of the sister town, a story of one long succession of struggles against the two enemies, the sea and the French. Although the place was a natural stronghold by reason of its unique formation, yet, after a time, the necessity for artificial works was felt, and in the twelfth century a small tower, afterwards known as the Ypres, was constructed near the top of the southward cliffs, a square structure of two stories with a circular turret at each angle. A few years afterwards, in the reign of Richard the First, licence was granted for the building of a town wall; and still later, in the reign of Edward the Third, the fortifications were completed by the building of a gateway with portcullis at the north-east end of the town.

These fortifications were rendered necessary by the *inning* of the shallows which separated Rye from the mainland, the sea having set to work, with the true ironic touch, depositing shingle where salt water was essential, and irrupting where it was most unwelcome. And, sure enough, as the one enemy did its worst, filling in the harbour and making access to the little hill more easy, so the other enemy took advantage of the facilities offered, and the raids of the French gradually became more frequent and more severe. In the fourteenth century things were parlous for the island town. When it was not the turn of Winchelsea, Rye suffered, and vice versa. They set upon the town in 1337 with no great success, but in 1360 they spoiled both Hastings and Rye. Immediately after the death of Edward they came again, and "within five hours brought it wholly into ashes, with the church that was there of a wonderful beauty, conveying away four of the richest of the towne and slaying sixty-six; left not above eight in the towne. Forty-two hogsheads of wine they carried thence to the ships with the rest of their booty, and left the towne desolate."

In 1378 the men of the Cinque Ports took some sort of revenge, according to the following interesting account in Fuller's *Worthies of*

England: "May never French land on this shore, to the losse of the English! But if so sad an accident should happen, send them our Sussexians no worse success than their ancestors of Rye and Winchelsey had, 1378, in the reign of Richard the Second, when they embarked for Normandy: for in the night they entered a town called Peter's Port, took all such prisoners who were able to pay ransome, and safely returned home without losse, and with much rich spoil; and amongst the rest they took out of the steeple the bells, and brought them into England, bells which the French had taken formerly from these towns, and which did afterwards ring the more merrily, restored to their proper place, with addition of much wealth to pay for the cost of their recovery." But their triumph was short-lived, for in 1380 the place was again burned, despite the wall. Comparative quiet then reigned till 1448, when the last and most terrible invasion occurred. Then, according to Jeake, Rye was entirely burned, with the exception of the Landgate, the walls of the parish church, Ypres Tower, and the so-called Chapel of the Carmelite Friars in Watchbell Street. The town was devastated to such an extent that it was unable to furnish its quota of ships to the navy.

Then the sea encroached once more, and, washing away the cliffs on the east, destroyed the walls built under commission of Richard the First; and such was the condition of the town that Chaucer could write:

"As many another town is payrid and y-lassid
Within these few years, as we mow se at eye
Lo, Sirs, here fast by Wynchelse and Ry".

Folks discovered that by skilful artificial drainage they could assist the inning, and so obtain an additional field at the extremity of their rightly-acquired land. In 1724 we have Defoe writing: "By digging Ditches, and making Drains there are now Fields and Meadows where antiently was nothing but Water. By this means Ships of but a middle Size cannot come to any convenient distance near the Town, whereas formerly the largest Vessels, and even whole Fleets together could anchor just by the Rocks on which the Town stands."

But still, despite its struggles--perhaps by reason of them--Rye has always managed to carry on. It has had its systole and diastole of success; but, unlike Winchelsea, it has never given up the fight. Periods there have been when every hand has seemed against it; but times there have been too--the Commonwealth, for instance--when the town has enjoyed a compensating prosperity. It has fought for its existence, and it has survived; and there are no more apt words concerning the two

Antient Towns than those of Coventry Patmore: "Winchelsea is a town in a trance, a sunny dream of centuries ago, but Rye is a bit of the Old World living on in happy ignorance of the New".

At Winchelsea the church is the centre of everything: you cannot move a hundred yards without coming into sight of it. But you might walk round and about Rye all day and not notice it. Shut away at the top of the hill, behind and away from all the everyday business of life, in its isolation it somewhat resembles a cathedral. But there the resemblance stops: there is no cathedral atmosphere. True, there is a quiet in the square, but it is not the cold ghostly hush of the close or the cloister. Instead, all is sunlight and warmth. The walls are grey, the buttresses are grey, the tombs are grey, but it is a warm familiar colour, at one with the red of the lichen-grown roofs, in full harmony with the surrounding mosaic of colour.

RYE CHURCH

Rye church stands at the top of the hill, behind and away from all the everyday business of life. Its walls are grey, but it is a warm familiar colour, at one with the red of the lichen-covered roofs.

(*See page 54*)

Just below the churchyard, in the south-east corner, the Ypres (or, as it is called locally, the Wipers) Tower still stands, a squat, heavy-looking building, not altogether beautiful; and at the other end of the town the Landgate, the sole survivor of the town's five portals. Between these two, dotted about here and there in the winding, cobble-stoned streets, are buildings of great beauty, some unfortunately modernized on the outside. One is the old rubble-stone building in Watchbell Street, commonly known as the Carmelite Friary. It is an interesting specimen of a small mediaeval hall with chambers below, but its association with the order is now pretty generally recognized as a mistake. Steep little Mermaid Street--perhaps the most beautiful of all the quaint turnings--has two notable buildings, the Old Hospital and the Mermaid Inn. The Hospital is a fine timbered structure with huge gables. The Inn is a Tudor building, surrounding a tiny court. Little is to be seen from the road; but inside it is a charming old-world place, with latticed windows and massive oak beams, fine panelling and great fireplaces. In the stately red house at the head of the street Mr. Henry James for many years found inspiration for his wonderful studies of modern temperaments,--about as remote as possible from the atmosphere of the quaint little grass-grown street. Perhaps the most interesting of all the buildings is the Old Flushing Inn. It possesses some fine oakwork, but the greatest attraction is the quaint mural painting in imitation of tapestry, covering the whole of one wall, and dating from 1574. In olden days the place was a popular rendezvous among gentlemen of the "free trade", for in the rear it possessed a courtyard which extended right to the edge of the cliff--at that point practically vertical and about sixty feet high--and it was a simple matter to beach a boat just below.

In High Street, almost facing the turning which leads up to the church, is a dark red-brick building of the seventeenth century: this is Pocock's Grammar School, which readers of Thackeray will remember as the place where Denis Duval was sent to be educated. A little farther along we come to Conduit Hill, in which is situate the Ancient Monastery of the Austin Friars--a fair building, possessing that rare thing, flamboyant tracery. If the ghosts of the little brothers of bygone days ever return to their former haunts, they must be deeply grieved or intensely amused, for the building has been everything from a malt-house to a Salvation Army barracks.

As we leave the town a flood of questions surges into the brain, perhaps never to be answered. Why is it there is such an attraction about Rye? Why will men and women travel half across the world to see these crooked streets once more? Why should the very mention of the name conjure up such haunting memories of the past? There is very little in the place that is actually old--a gateway, one or two houses, a small tower, a church--yet the impression is one of remotest antiquity.

BODIAM

When in 1377, following on other successful raids, the French descended on Rye and sacked and fired the town, it became evident that Hastings could no longer afford sufficient protection to that stretch of the coast, or to the important river valley leading thence inwards; and the necessity for another stronghold was immediately realized. Thus did Bodiam come into existence.

It so happened that, at the moment when the defenceless condition of the Rother became apparent, there had come into the district a knight well skilled in all the military arts, one Edward Dalyngrigge, a member of an old Sussex family and brother to the sheriff of the county. Dalyngrigge had spent many years in France, and taken part in numerous expeditions, some of them scarcely creditable. Following a fierce but capable warrior, one ready for almost any emergency, he had learned not only the art of the soldier but also the science of the castellan. Now, Sir Edward was married to Elizabeth Wardeux, the heiress of the manor of Bodiam, and therefore possessed of the old moated manor-house some distance from the river. Consequently, in virtue of the necessity of the times, Sir Edward had little difficulty in extracting the licence to build a suitable castle.

BODIAM CASTLE

The castle is a ruin--a mere empty shell--but outwardly its towers and walls rise sheer from the lily-covered waters of the moat in a fine state of preservation.

(*See page 59*)

The site selected was the left bank of the Rother, at a spot some thirty feet above the level of the water. Partly by excavation, partly by damming up, a great reservoir was constructed, 525 feet from north to south and 330 feet from east to west; and in the centre an island was left, a little over an acre in extent. On this island the castle was erected; and the basin was flooded from a little stream which the premeditating builder had previously diverted and dammed. Northward the ground rose pretty steeply from the moat, a circumstance which seems to detract somewhat from the strength of the castle, till we remember that the planning and building were done in the days before artillery had become the deciding factor in warfare. Southwards the ground fell away to the river, and because of this much doubt has been cast on the efficacy of the stronghold. It has been pointed out frequently that an investing army would have had little difficulty in piercing the bank of the basin; but there was no mediaeval siege whereby its strength might have been tested.

The castle was built in the form of a parallelogram, after the French model, with four strong curtain walls protected at the angles by boldly projecting round towers, 54 feet high and 29 in diameter. Three of the curtain walls had intermediate square towers, while the fourth, that on the northern side, had a double tower flanking the great gateway. Between this deep and well-protected portal and the land stood an octagonal platform on which was built an advance work, or barbican, the intervening spaces being bridged by drawbridges. Thus was the way into the castle strongly held by a succession of defences.

As we approach the castle now from any side, it is difficult to realize that it is a ruin--a mere empty shell. Outwardly its towers and walls rise sheer from the lily-covered waters of the moat in a fine state of preservation: curtain walls, round towers, square towers, battlements,--all are there as in the days that were. True, the drawbridges are gone, and of the barbican only a fragment remains; but of the great donjon itself nothing appears to be missing until--until we cross the causeway where once the drawbridge rose and fell, and so come to the interior. Then do we realize the antiquity of the place; for everything has crumbled to dust, leaving just here and there a suggestion of what has been--a window, a buttress, a fireplace. Lines from Lord Thurlow's sonnet come to mind:

"Thou hast had thy prime,
And thy full vigour, and the eating harms
Of age have robb'd thee of thy warlike charms,
And placed thee here, an image in my rhyme;
The owl now haunts thee, and oblivion's plant,

The creeping ivy, has o'er-veil'd thy towers;
And Rother looking up with eye askant,
Recalling to his mind thy brighter hours,
Laments the time, when fair and elegant
Beauty first laugh'd from out thy joyous bowers".

From the ruined fragments we mentally reconstruct the scene of the interior, the single courtyard in the centre, the two-story buildings all around with the chapel going up through both stories, and we note with astonishment the comparative convenience and comfort of the arrangements of the compact little fortalice.

Certainly Bodiam (or Bojum, as it is pronounced locally) is the most picturesque castle in the south, many say in the whole, of England. Nestling in the little valley, surrounded by luxuriant greenery, it has not the impressive grandeur of the stronghold flaunting its strength at the head of some precipitous cliff, or bidding defiance to the hungry seas, but it has a beauty more at one with the spirit of Sussex and the south.

And yet, Bodiam is a place of inviolate mystery. You can fall in love with its unique situation, with its delightful lily-covered, bird-haunted setting; you can be impressed by its note of artistic completeness; but always there is something of loneliness and horror about the place. Its walls are grey, but not with the grey of other castles. It is a cold, pitiless grey, no matter how the sun shine, no matter how the water throw up again the quivering light. There is a shudder in the air on the blithest summer day. Perhaps it is that places, no less than men, gradually take upon them a personality. If that is so, then surely Bodiam has taken the personality of its old founder, Dalyngrigge, a bleak enough man, if records speak truly, a man dark in deed and light of word.

At Bodiam we leave this Enchanted Garden; and as we go we begin to wonder that a place so rich in memories and in charm has no representative poet, or, indeed, school of poets. Sussex in general seems to have been sadly neglected by our singers. Kipling has probably sung most in her praises; but even for Kipling the great chalk downs have always been Sussex. And most of our other poets--Habberton Lulham, Arthur F. Bell, Rosamund Watson, Wilfred Scawen Blunt--have followed in his steps. Only occasionally has one ventured down into the marshlands and the low rolling hills and the little river valleys in quest of beauty. And yet beauty indescribable is here for the seeking. Probably the poet who knows us best is Ford Maddox Hueffer, whose volume, *The Cinque Ports,* contains some magnificent word-pictures of these happy little hills and dales, and whose novel, *The 'Half Moon'*, gives such a faithful picture of Rye of ancient days. The following fragment from one of his poems gives the marsh in all its beauty:

"Up here, where the air's very clear,
And the hills slope away nigh down to the bay,
It is very like Heaven....
"For the sea's wine-purple and lies half asleep
In the sickle of the shore and, serene in the west,
Lion-like purple and brooding in the even,
Low hills lure the sun to rest.
"Very like Heaven.... For the vast marsh dozes,
And waving plough-lands and willowy closes
Creep and creep up the soft south steep;
In the pallid North the grey and ghostly downs do fold away.
And, spinning spider-threadlets down the sea, the sea-lights dance,
And shake out a wavering radiance...."

We close with a short passage from the volume on the Cinque Ports. It was written concerning the old military canal at Winchelsea, but in its brooding spirit of contentment it applies but little less to the whole of this wonderful area. "Nowhere is one so absolutely alone; but nowhere do inanimate things--the water plants and the lichens on the stiles--afford so much company. It must not be hurried through, or it is a dull, flat stretch. But linger and saunter through it, and you are caught by the heels in a moment. You will catch a malady of tranquillity--a kind of idle fever that will fall on you in distant places for years after. And one must needs be the better, in times of storm and stress, for that restful remembrance."

THE END

Printed in Dunstable, United Kingdom

73429208R20030